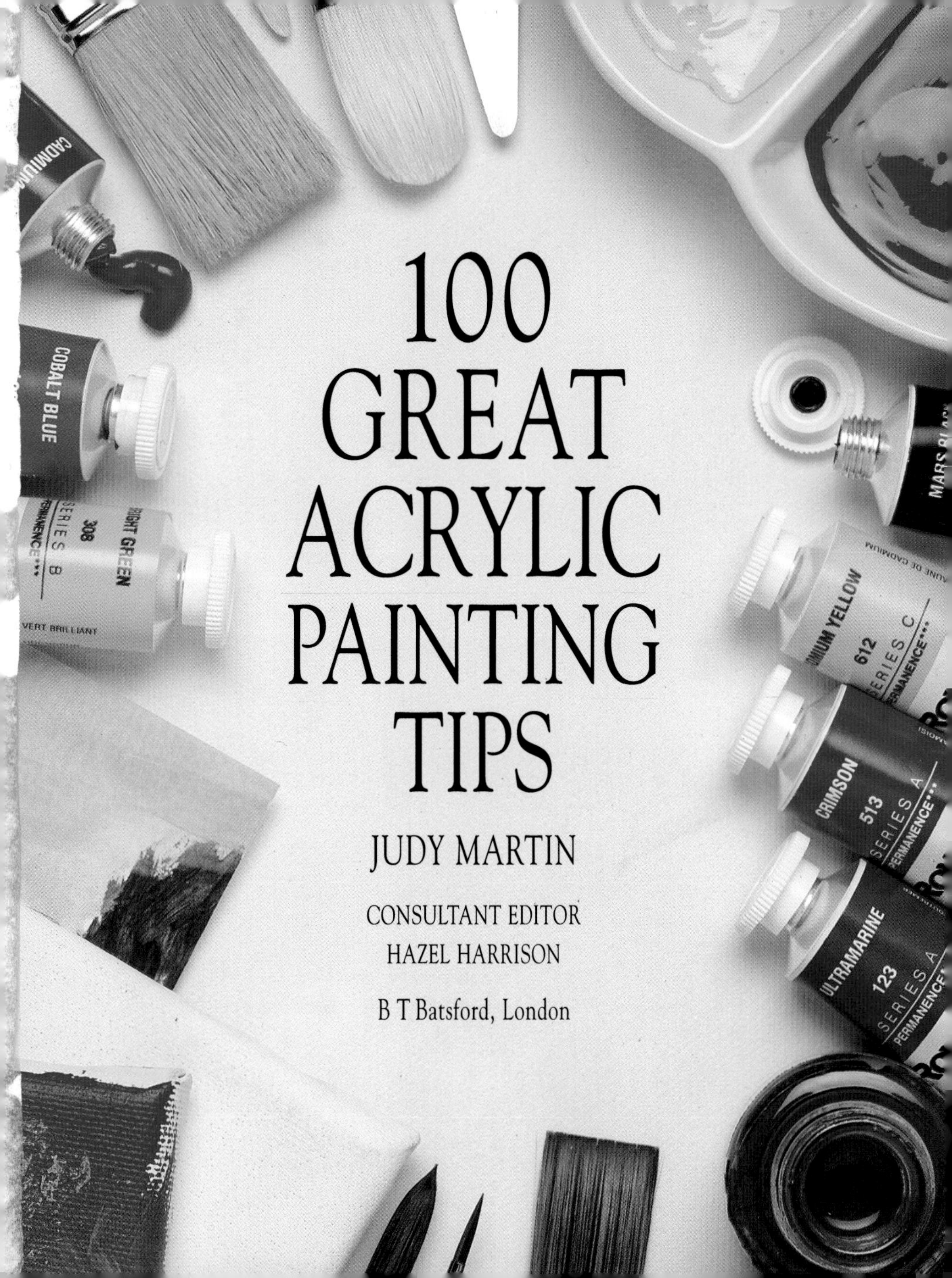

100 GREAT ACRYLIC PAINTING TIPS

JUDY MARTIN

CONSULTANT EDITOR
HAZEL HARRISON

B T Batsford, London

A QUARTO BOOK

First published in Great Britain by
B. T. Batsford Ltd
4 Fitzhardinge Street
London W1H 0AH

ISBN 0-7134-7911-6

A catalogue record for this book is available from the British Library.

This book was designed and produced by
Quarto Publishing plc
The Old Brewery
6 Blundell Street
London N7 9BH

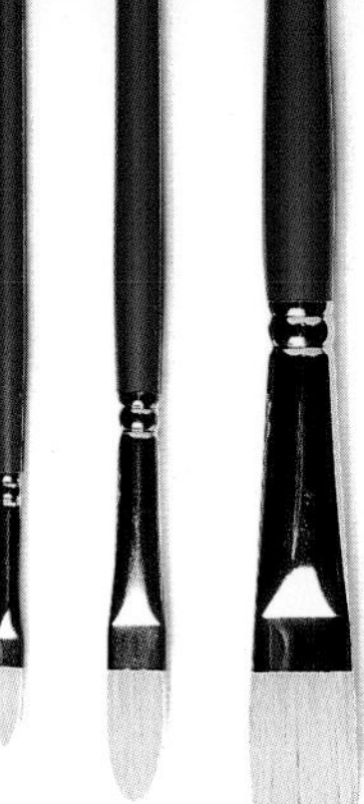

Contents

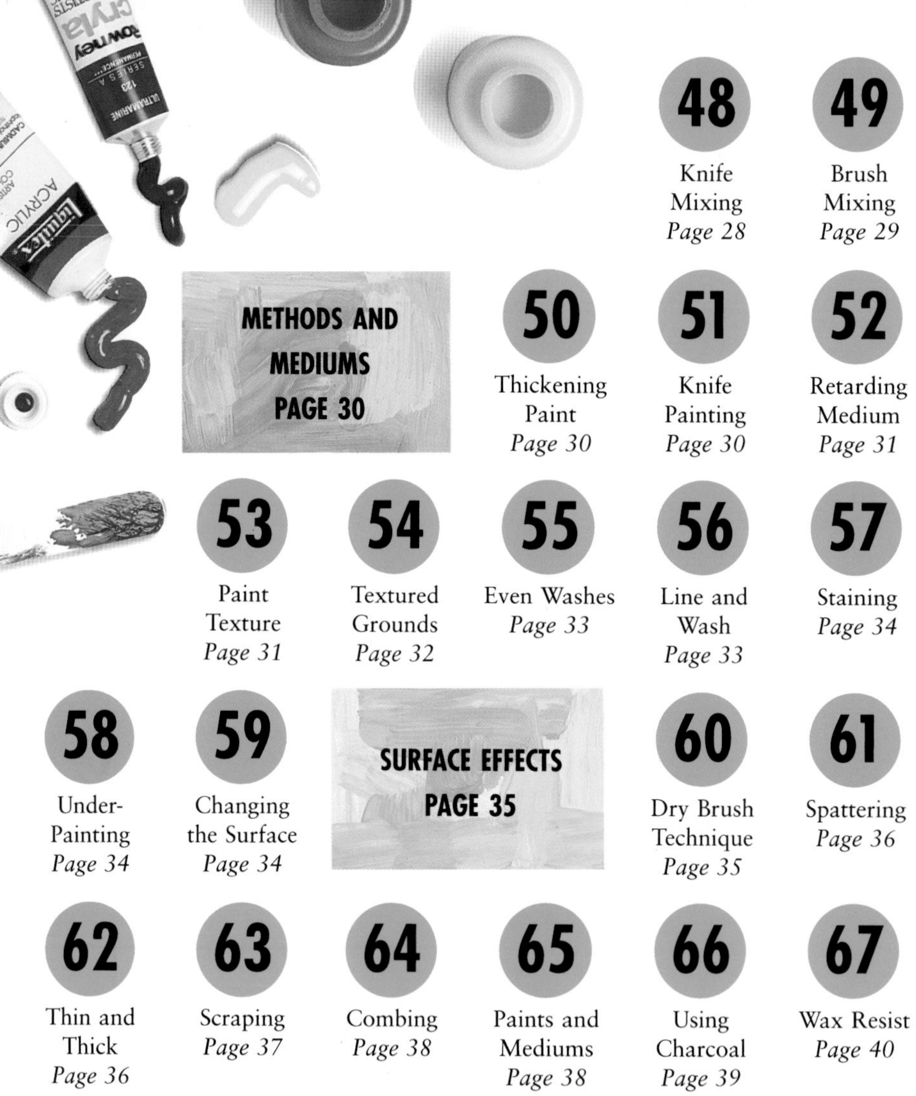

INTRODUCTION by Hazel Harrison

WHEN YOU LOOK at a finished painting you can nearly always tell whether it has been done in watercolour, pastels or oils. Acrylic, however, tends to hide its identity simply because it is a medium that can be used in so many different ways. This high degree of versatility is part of its charm, but it can lead to a rather sterile approach, where acrylic is used to imitate oils, watercolours or gouache paints instead of being appreciated for its own special qualities. Because acrylic is a new medium in art-history terms, having only been around since the mid-20th century, there is no "official" body of techniques associated with it, as there is for the other painting media. And there can never really be one because you can do more or less anything you like with it. You can paint on paper, canvas or board, use the paint thin or thick, apply it with knives or brushes, combine it with other media, stick pieces of paper into it for collage effects – the list is virtually endless. This is why *100 Great Acrylic Painting Tips* is so valuable; it does not attempt to provide a full course, but it opens your eyes to just a few of the things you can do. If you go to a painting class, or buy a standard book on acrylic painting you will learn how one artist goes about using acrylics, but you may never explore the wider possibilities or conduct your own experiments.

The book contains a wealth of exciting techniques for you to try out at your leisure, but it does not neglect practical advice. As anyone who has used the medium will know, acrylic dries very fast, which can cause you to waste expensive paint and ruin good brushes. But a little know-how, combined with self-discipline, can prevent this, and you can also save money by working on inexpensive surfaces such as paper, or "canvases" made by sticking old sheets onto board.

100 Great Acrylic Painting Tips is intended for dipping into rather than reading from cover to cover at one go, and is divided into chapters for easy access to the kind of information you want. For advice on paints, surfaces, brushes and palettes, and help on choosing and mixing colours, turn to the first sections, and refer to the later ones for inspiration on techniques, special effects, and methods for dealing with subject-related problems. Had you thought, for example, of using masking tape to keep the edges of buildings straight, or painting little sky patches over the foliage of trees with opaque paint? There is even a short section on making corrections and alterations, so if you have a painting that hasn't quite worked, use it as a learning tool and see if you can improve it by overpainting or laying coloured glazes.

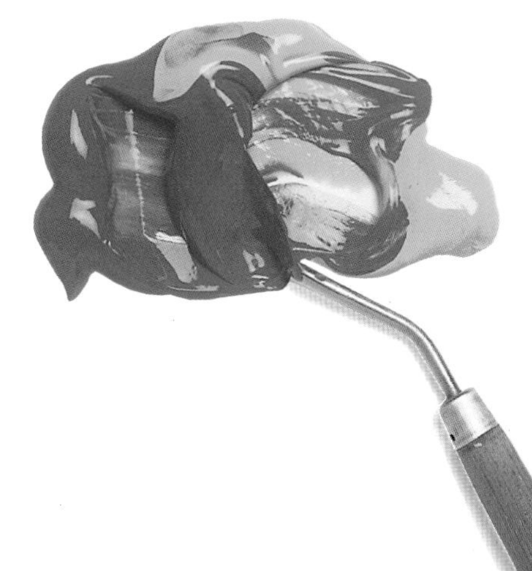

PAINTS

Starting out with a new medium can be bewildering; without some guidance you may have little idea of what to buy. This section provides practical advice which will help the beginner to make wise initial purchases, while some of the hints will give the "old hand" food for thought.

1

PAINT TEXTURE The various brands of acrylic paints vary in texture, from thick and buttery to smooth and relatively fluid. It is worth trying two or three to see whether one suits your painting methods better than another. You can mix or layer different types to use up any odd tubes you have collected, but it is advisable to do samples to test their compatibility before combining them in a finished painting.

2

PAINT QUALITY Acrylics are most widely available in tubes. Free-flow types are also packaged in jars, providing greater quantity but sometimes in a more restricted colour range. White is often sold in a large-sized tube in addition to the standard size, because it is used up more quickly than other colours.

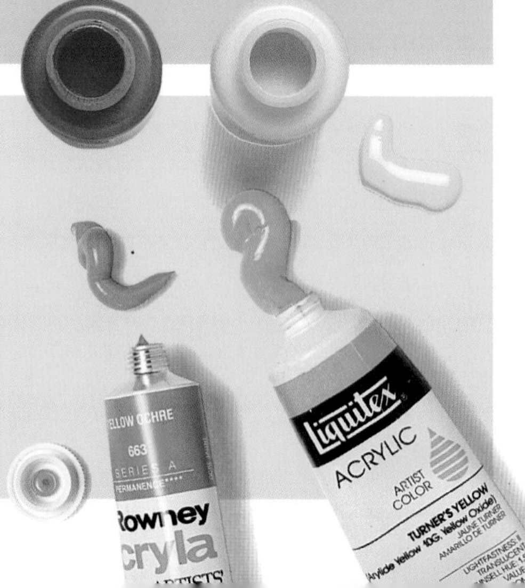

3

DRYING TESTS Acrylics dry much more rapidly than other types of paint, but drying rate can vary according to the absorbency of the surface you are painting on. Try making some colour doodles on a small offcut of paper, board or canvas, to see how quickly the colours dry. Test the paint in different consistencies straight from the tube, just moistened with water, and brushed out in a wet wash.

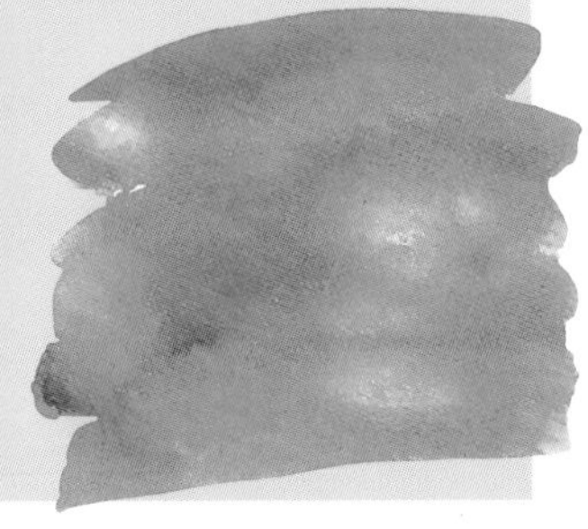

4

DRYING IN LAYERS Acrylic paint gradually seals the working surface, forming a durable "plastic skin" as it dries. As you build up your colour effects, you may find that later layers are slower-drying, because the surface beneath is no longer absorbent. Be careful not to overwork each stage when this happens, or the colours will muddy.

5

MIXABLE PAINTS Some types of acrylic are sold in the form of basic mediums together with liquid pigments or colour pastes, which you can use to mix up your own colours. Put them into screw-top jars and they will store well long-term. This is useful if you do large-scale work, or if you are sharing costs between members of a painting class.

Some established oil paint manufacturers have begun producing acrylic paints like those pictured below.

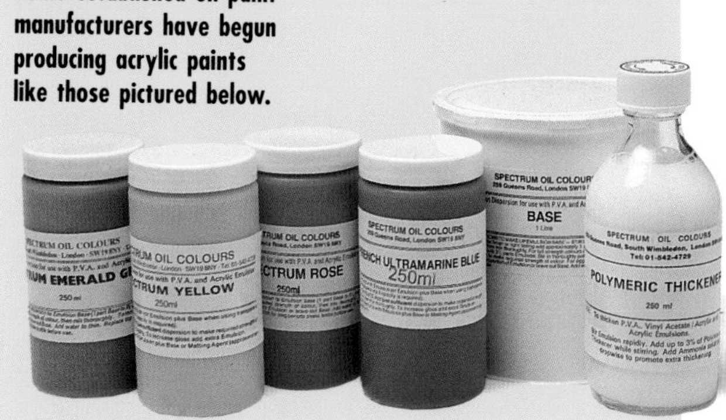

SURFACES

One of the beauties of acrylics is that you can paint on more or less anything, even newspaper, so you need not spend a great deal in the early trying-out stages. If you find you like working on canvas, you can save money by stretching your own, even recycling old sheets by sticking them down on board.

6

ECONOMY PAPERS You can paint with acrylics on all kinds of paper. Ordinary brown wrapping paper, shelf paper and even newspaper can be recycled for practising your brushwork, experimenting with colour mixes etc.

7

PAPER TEXTURE On a smooth-surfaced support, such as cartridge or coated paper, the paint rapidly seals the surface and "sits" on top. The colours can start to skid around as you add to the layers, making coverage uneven, so you should expect to make use of directional brushmarks. Watercolour papers with a pronounced grain grip the paint more firmly and the paint texture remains fully workable for longer.

In "View of San Francisco" (detail) Jacquie Turner has used smooth watercolour paper.

8

STRETCHING PAPER Lightweight watercolour papers buckle when wetted by the paint, but will always dry out flat again if stretched beforehand. Soak the paper either by immersing it in clean water or by sponging on both sides. Lay it on a drawing board and tape down each edge in turn with gummed paper tape. Leave it to dry naturally on a flat surface. If you leave it propped up, water drains to the lower edge and may loosen the tape.

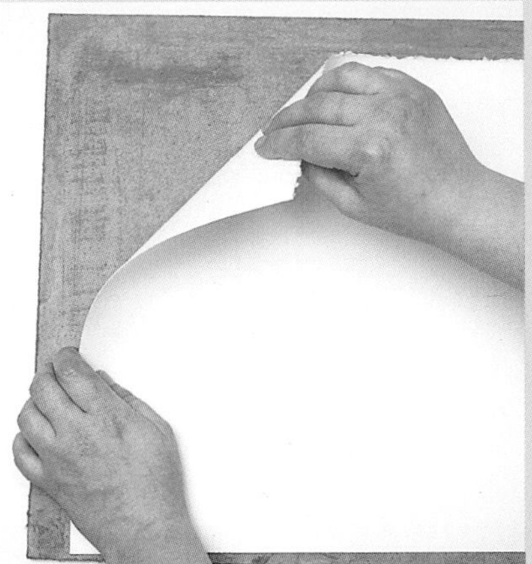

Wet the paper on both sides and place it carefully on the board.

Damp the gummed tape and stick it around the edges, allowing an overlap of at least 1.5cm (½in).

9

USING CARDBOARD

Cardboard is a useful surface for acrylic painting, and often comes free – you may find pieces from commercial packaging, or the back cover of a used-up paper pad. Look for a firm, fibrous texture rather than cardboard composed of paper layers; the top layer may peel up when wetted by the paint.

10

PREPARED SURFACES Canvas boards are relatively expensive but have the advantages of being lightweight, self-supporting and easy to frame. Pre-stretched canvases are also available. Check that the type you buy is suitable for acrylics; most are now usable for work in acrylics or oils, but acrylics will not adhere to a surface specially primed for oils.

11

HARDBOARD This is an inexpensive surface which has the advantage of rigidity. The smooth side is normally used, and can be made less slippery by light sanding followed by a coat of matt medium or acrylic gesso. For a really heavy texture, try using the rough side.

12

STRETCHING CANVAS You can buy both prepared and "raw" canvas by the metre. Assemble the stretchers, cut the canvas to size, allowing for a turnover, and tack or staple it to the back of the stretchers, pulling it taut and taking care to keep the grain straight.

Assemble the stretchers and cut the canvas to size.

Staple or tack first one long side and then the other.

Staple each side before folding the corners over.

13

ECONOMY CANVAS You can use pieces of an old sheet or pillowcase instead of canvas, "stretching" it by sticking it down on the smooth side of hardboard, with an overlap of about 2.5cm (1in) taken around the back. For light fabrics, use acrylic medium, and for heavier ones PVA glue thinned with water to about half and half.

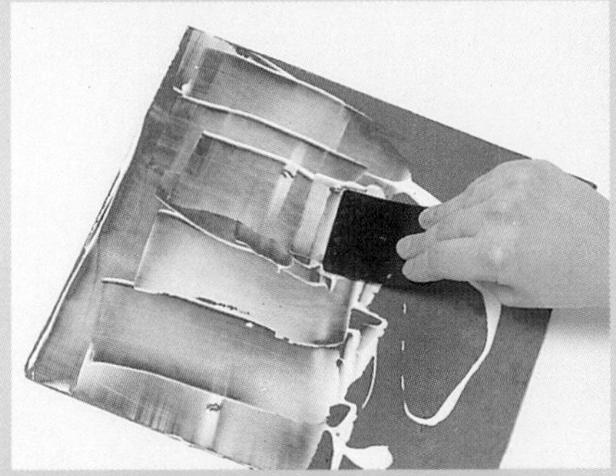

Cover the board with medium. Use a brush, or a spreader to give a thicker application.

Place the glued side down on the canvas, apply more glue around the back edges; fold over.

14

PRIMING Untreated fabric is absorbent, so canvases are usually primed before use. Give them at least two coats of acrylic gesso, or if you like the natural colour of the canvas, seal it with matt medium.

Canvas is primed with acrylic gesso. Use it thickly and scrub it into the fabric, or it will "sit" only on top of the grain. Leave to dry before applying a second coat.

15

COLOURED GROUND Working on a white surface makes it hard to assess the initial colours. Primed canvas or hardboard is often given an overall tint in a mid-toned neutral colour such as ochre or grey. You can pre-tint watercolour paper in the same way.

BRUSHES AND PALETTES

However much you enjoy working with acrylics you may love them less when you have ruined expensive brushes or a good wooden oil-painting palette by letting the paint dry on them. This chapter, which combines advice on the best choices of brushes and palettes with hints on equipment care, will help you avoid such occurrences.

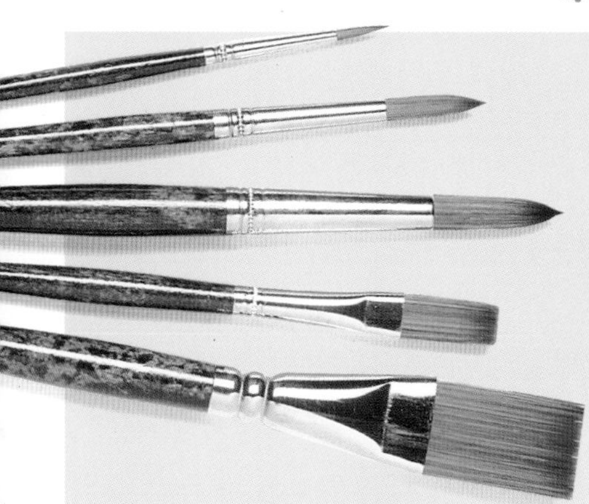

16

ACRYLIC BRUSHES Manufacturers make brush ranges specially designed for working with acrylic paints. These are made with synthetic rather than animal hairs and are available in round or flat shapes and in varying sizes. The quality of the brush tip is smooth but resilient for manipulating thick and thin paint.

17

BRUSH ACTION When you buy a brush, test out its versatility with some simple brush sketching. Try variations on using the tip and side, turn a flat brush onto its edges and corners. Apply different pressures and create thick and thin strokes, dashes or dabs and long travelling marks.

18

BRISTLE BRUSHES The hoghair brushes traditionally used for oil painting are also suited to acrylics. Their toughness makes them useful for applying rough, heavy or coarse painting effects, such as dry brushing and impasto.

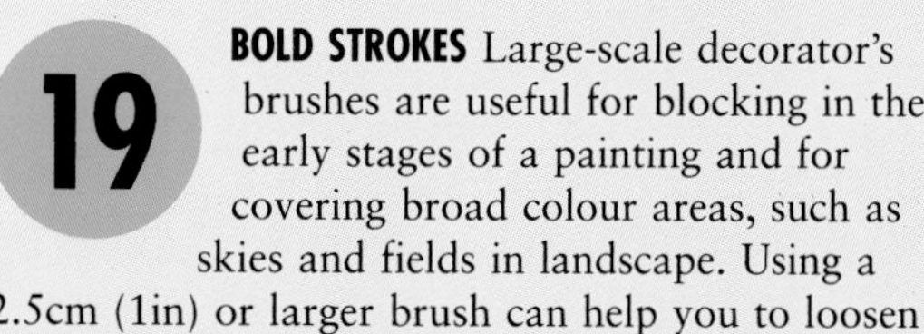

19

BOLD STROKES Large-scale decorator's brushes are useful for blocking in the early stages of a painting and for covering broad colour areas, such as skies and fields in landscape. Using a 2.5cm (1in) or larger brush can help you to loosen up your technique. By experimenting with pushing and pulling the brush through fluid paint, you can discover interesting ways of blending and texturing the colour.

In Paul Powis's "Late Afternoon" (detail), the broad brushstrokes, which suggest shapes and forms without literal description, are an important part of the image.

20 THOROUGH CLEANING

Dried acrylic ruins brushes. Be scrupulous about rinsing your brush every time you complete a colour application, keep brushes moist throughout a working session and wash them out well at the end. The most common cause of damage is paint collecting at the heel of the brush above the metal ferrule, causing gradual stiffening, so pay special attention to washing that part right through.

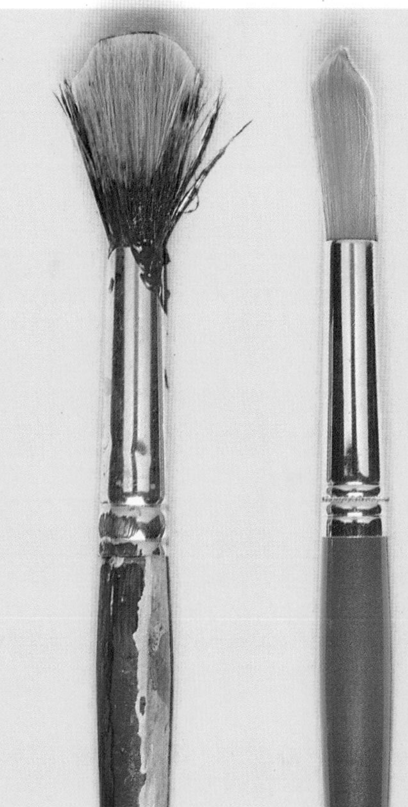

21

OLD BRUSHES If you have let paint dry in your brush, it can be loosened by soaking in methylated spirits. The brush shape and texture will be damaged, but many artists like to keep old, worn brushes for creating scrubbed and scumbled textures, saving hard wear on newer brushes.

22

STRAY BRISTLES A bristle or hair shed into the paint as you work will become firmly trapped as soon as the colour begins to dry. Keep an eye out for shed hairs and quickly flick them out of the wet paint with an upward and outward motion of the brush tip.

23 RESHAPING A BRUSH

If your brush has begun to splay or shed hairs, wash it out thoroughly and shake off excess moisture, then take the tip between your fingers and carefully stroke and press it back into shape, teasing out loose hairs as you do so.

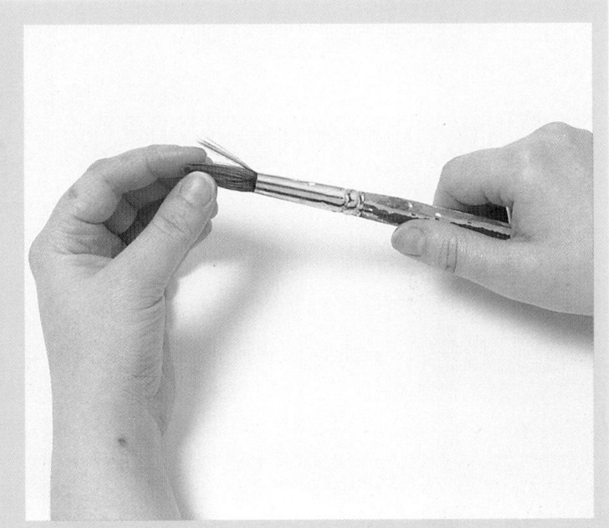

24

KNIFE WORK Painting knives and palette knives are invaluable for working into heavy acrylics; making good use of knives can help you to prolong the life of your brushes. A flat, spatulate palette knife is the tool for mixing the colours before you apply them. A painting knife has an angled shaft so you can manipulate the blade on the surface while keeping your hand clear of the painting.

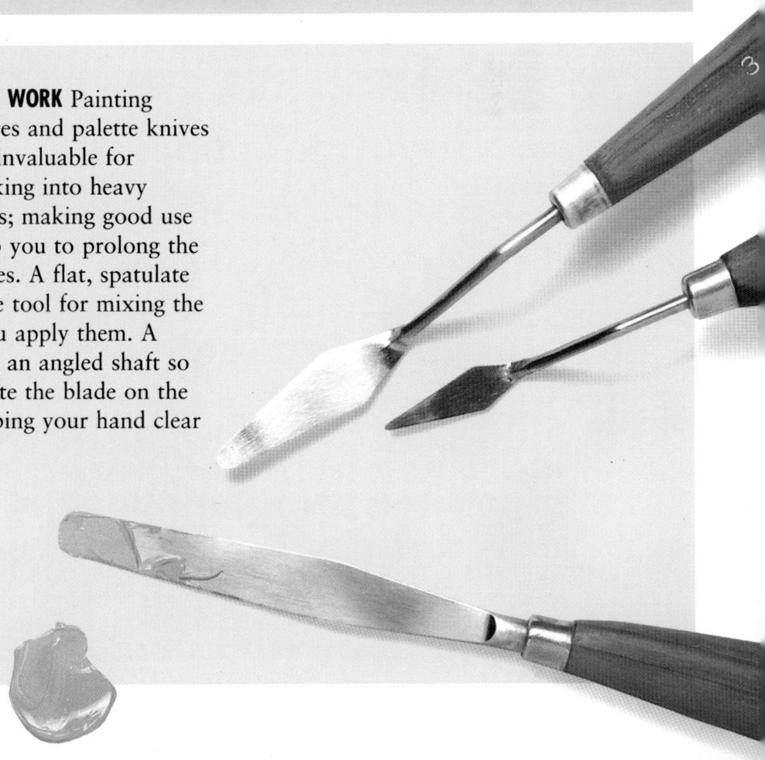

25

SCRAPERS Save old credit cards or telephone cards – they make very useful paint applicators for scraped and pasted textures, and also give you a clean, broad edge for scraping off wet colour when you have made an error.

In Peter Adams's "Board Street, Alresford" (detail), paint has been scraped onto hardboard and colours layered over each other.

26

PERMANENT PALETTES You can use a purpose-made plastic or ceramic palette for acrylic paint, but many artists improvise with cheaper items. For long-term use, the material must be non-absorbent. A piece of plastic-coated wood is fine, as is an old plate or a plain sheet of glass, the thicker the better. Cover the edges with insulating tape to avoid cutting yourself accidentally.

27

TEAR-OFF PALETTES You can buy tear-off paper palettes, but an old telephone directory provides a cheap alternative for quick painting sessions. Lay out and mix your colours on the top sheet. When the colours get muddy, or you have used up all the paint, tear off the top few pages and start again.

Old telephone directories

Tear-off palette

28

COLOUR QUANTITIES Acrylics start to harden quite fast once exposed to air. To avoid waste, when you put them out on the palette, start with small quantities and add to them as you need. If a blob of paint has started to dry, peel off the rubbery "skin" so you do not brush shreds of it into still-wet colours.

29

MOIST PAINT To keep palette colours moist you can use a specially designed "reservoir" palette, in which a damp underlayer continuously supplies the paint with enough moisture to keep it workable, or you can make your own version. You need a plastic or metal tray, a piece of capillary matting (as used to keep potted plants moist), a piece of absorbent paper such as cartridge or newsprint, and a same-size piece of cooking parchment or thin tracing paper. To prime the palette, soak the matting for 15 minutes and squeeze it out so that it is moist, not wet, then put it in the tray base and layer in the paper and parchment or tracing paper.

Allow the capillary matting to absorb the water, then lay the cartridge paper on top.

Finally, place the cooking parchment or tracing paper on top. To keep moist between working sessions, cover the whole with cling film.

30

AVOID WASTAGE If you are using a conventional palette and have to leave blobs of paint already laid out for a short time only, thoroughly wet a rag or kitchen cloth, wring it out and drape it lightly over the palette.

31

REMOVING DRIED PAINT Dried acrylic on a plastic, glass or ceramic palette can be loosened by running warm water over it. The paint skin softens and begins to lift, so you can peel or scrape it off.

COLOURS

It is wise to begin with a small range of colours, as this helps you build up the skills of identifying the colours you see and mixing them accurately. This section explains which colours you must have, and gives hints on colour mixing and on methods of modifying over-bright colours.

32 WHITE AND BLACK

You need to include white in your starter palette for heightening bright colours and mixing pale tints. Black can be used for darkening colours and tones, but is not essential; some artists regard it as a deadening influence and prefer to mix their own "coloured blacks". Try this out with varying proportions of red, yellow and blue.

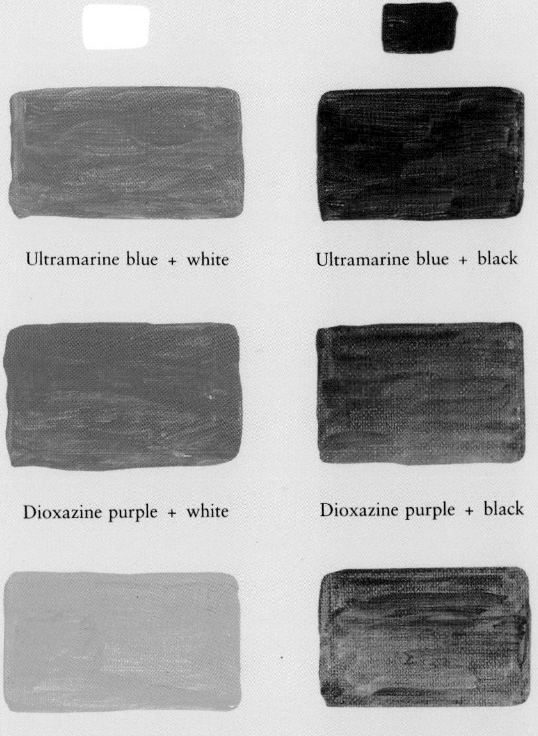

33

PRIMARY CHOICE In theory, you can mix all colours from only three – red, yellow and blue – but in practice it is not quite that simple, because there are different versions of these colours. In a limited palette, select two types of each, for example, cadmium red and crimson; cadmium yellow and lemon yellow; ultramarine and phthalo blue. Used in pairs, these give you many grades of secondary mixes – oranges, purples and greens – and by mixing two or more colours you can obtain subtler shades and neutral colours.

For this chart, the mix is in a ratio of 80% strength to 20% strength.

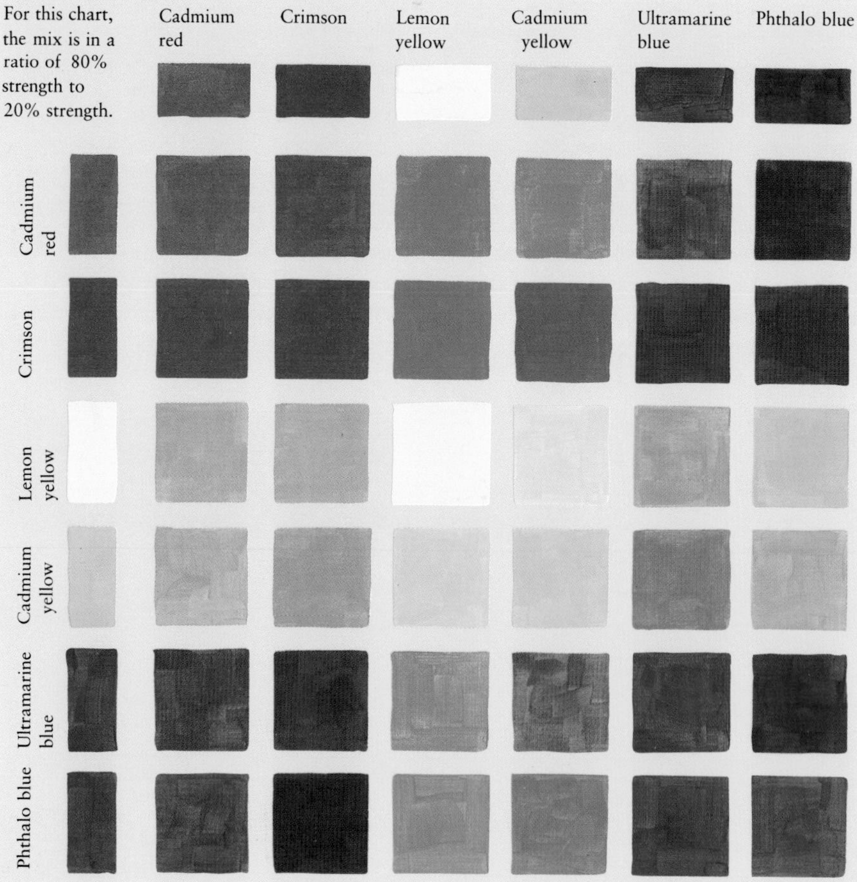

Cadmium red

Crimson

Lemon yellow

Cadmium yellow

Ultramarine blue

Phthalo blue

Cadmium red

Crimson

Lemon yellow

Cadmium yellow

Ultramarine blue

Phthalo blue

34

CHART YOUR MIXES If you buy a manufacturer's starter pack of acrylic colours, take the time to make your own colour chart for reference. Mix all of the colours in pairs; try out two of three variants with each pair, using equal and 3:1 proportions. Some results may surprise you, and you will find out whether particular colours can or cannot be mixed from your given range.

Brilliant mauves such as the shadows in Gerry Baptist's "Summer Day in Grimaud" (detail) are best achieved with tube purples.

35

EXTRA COLOURS Some colours, notably purples, are virtually impossible to mix satisfactorily. A tube of purple is a useful addition to your palette, both as a colour in its own right and as a good mixer. It is ideal for warming up townscape greys and beiges and is a versatile shading colour for landscape greens and blues.

36

CHECKING A MATCH When you think you have a correct mix for something in your subject, load the brush thickly with paint and hold it up in front of you against the "real-life" colour. This will quickly show you whether the overall character of the colour and the level of tone are accurate.

37

IDENTIFYING COLOURS Some colours are more difficult to mix than others, but it can be helpful to think your way through a checklist of points that will give you clues to the ingredients of your mix.

- What kind of colour is it?
- Is it light, mid-toned or dark?
- Which of my tube colours is nearest the main component?
- Does it have a distinct tinge of another colour – which of my tube colours is nearest to that?
- Is it warm or cool?
- Is it intense or subdued?

The colour swatches below show examples of how these principles can be applied.

Warm	Cool	Dark	Light	Colour bias
				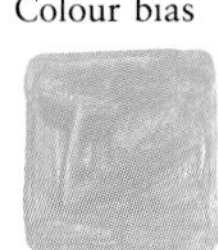
Cadmium red + black + white	Phthalocyanine green + black + white	Dioxazine purple + phthalocyanine green	White + lemon yellow + black	Lemon yellow (+ raw umber + white)

Cadmium yellow + white + dioxazine purple	Dioxazine purple + raw umber + white	Ultramarine blue + naphthol crimson	White + dioxazine purple + cadmium yellow	Ultramarine blue (+ raw umber + white)

38

ORDER OF MIXING When mixing a pale colour, start with the weakest ingredient, say, yellow or white. Then add the stronger colours such as red or blue in small quantities, building up gradually to the strength you require. If you start with a strong hue you will have to add much more of the mixer colour, wasting a lot of paint.

39 RECORDING MIXES

When you have mixed a colour that was specially difficult to achieve, take a minute to paint a patch on a spare piece of paper and note down the component colours that you used. Put the colour samples into a pocket file or scrapbook for later reference.

Alizarin crimson + cobalt blue + ivory black

40 BRIGHTER COLOURS

Adding white sometimes deadens the colour intensity. Borrow a trick from watercolour painting, and use transparent washes rather than opaque paint to build up the required hue. Thin colour allows the underlying white paper (or a ground of clean, fully dry white paint) to shine through, giving luminosity and freshness. This is often specially good for flower colours (pinks, violets, oranges and deep reds) that have a natural brilliance.

41

MODIFYING HUES Some acrylic colours are very strong and artificial-looking and are not always suitable for painting natural subjects. If you want to modify a hue quite subtly, try adding small touches of the more subdued earth colours – the muted browns and yellows. For example, mix burnt sienna into green, and yellow ochre into mauve.

Bright green

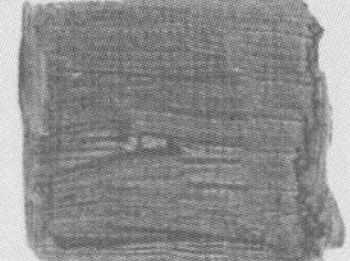

Bright green + burnt sienna

Bright green + red violet

43

BEAUTIFUL NEUTRALS Neutral greys and beiges need not be boring and dull. Try mixing unlike colours that neutralize each other but retain lively undertones. For example, mix crimson and Hooker's green; cadmium orange and ultramarine; cadmium yellow and deep violet. Titanium white is added to heighten and vary the tones.

42

KNOCKING BACK If one colour or area of the painting looks too bright, lay a thin glaze of a neutral colour over it. Use a large soft brush and dilute the paint either with plain water or with a mixture of water and acrylic medium, which gives a glossier effect.

A vivid purple, diluted with water, is laid over dry paint.

The effect was over-bright, so is modified with glazes of more muted hue.

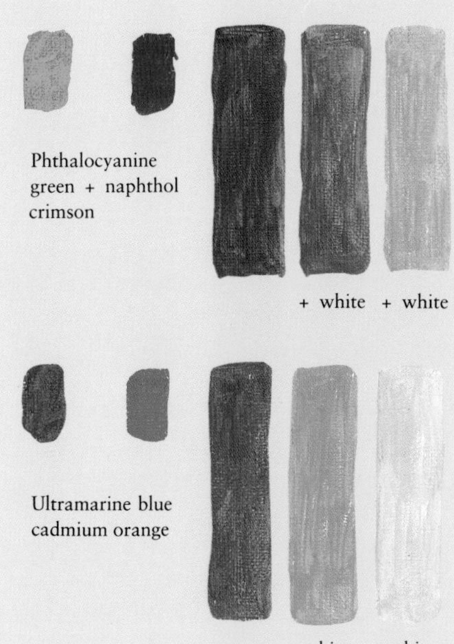

44 **INCREASING OPACITY** Some acrylic colours, though deep-toned, are relatively transparent and will not give flat, even coverage in one coat. A little added white increases the opacity without significantly altering the tone or intensity. This also brings out the colour of some dark shades of purple, blue and green, which otherwise become dulled as they dry.

45 **MIXING A WASH** When diluting thick colour to wash consistency, add the water in small amounts and brush it in thoroughly; keep working in a little more water at a time until you get the fluidity you want. If you add too much water in one go, the paint may separate into tiny blobs and particles that do not all disperse, and your wash will be streaky.

48 **KNIFE MIXING** If you are mixing thick acrylic colours, you may find it easiest to work them together on the palette with a knife. Don't just mash them together, as this can leave them partially unmixed, so the colour changes shade as you lay on the paint. Use a palette knife to scoop the colours up together and knead them on the palette; spread the paint to check for unblended streaks.

46 **LAYING OUT COLOURS** Set out your colours in the same order on your palette each time you start to paint. That way you can get used to finding the colour you need quickly, making it easier to create your colour mixes.

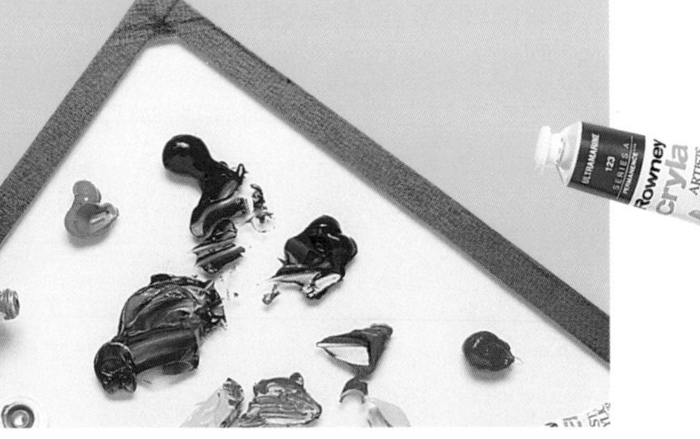

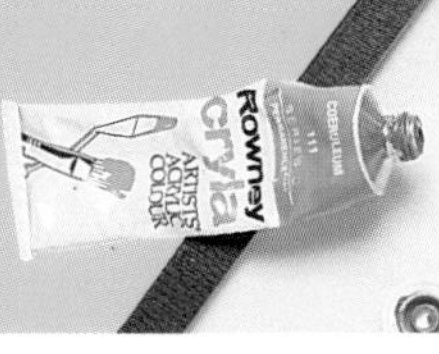

47 **BRUSHING OUT** Thick acrylic can be quite resistant and you may need to brush it out thoroughly on the palette to avoid transferring lumpy-textured colour onto the working surface. Use a springy, tough bristle- or synthetic-hair brush to work into the paint until it is smooth and malleable.

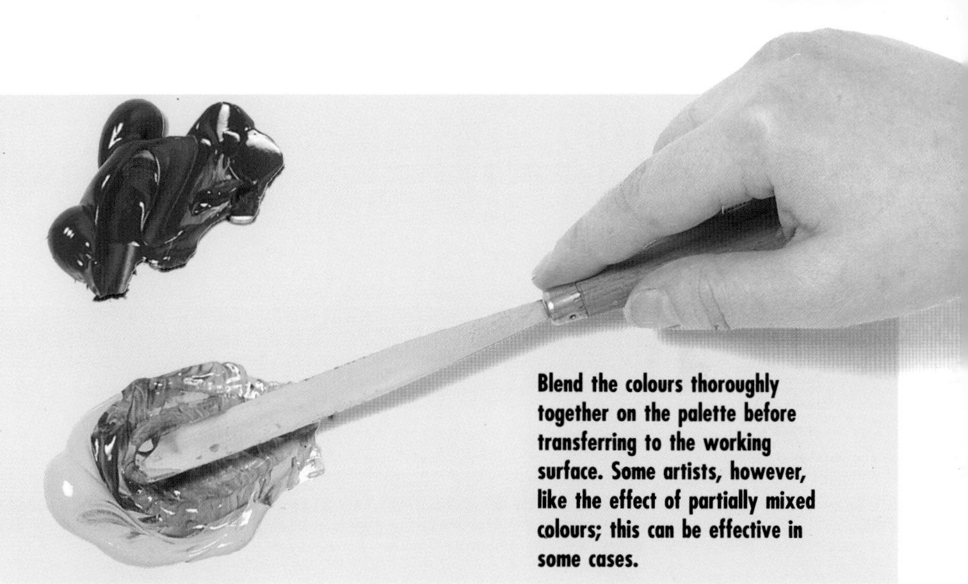

Blend the colours thoroughly together on the palette before transferring to the working surface. Some artists, however, like the effect of partially mixed colours; this can be effective in some cases.

49 BRUSH MIXING

When you mix colours together using a brush, you will find it ends up overloaded with paint. To squeeze out the excess colour, put it down flat on the palette and run the edge of a palette knife or plastic card down the bristles from base to tip.

METHODS AND MEDIUMS

Acrylic is the most versatile of all the painting media. You do not have to use it at tube consistency – you can thin it so that it resembles watercolour, bulk it out with special mediums for rich impasto effects, or even mix it with sand to produce textured effects. The tips on these pages will help you to experiment and discover your own methods.

50

THICKENING PAINT If you like to apply paint very thickly, consider buying one of the special "impasto" mediums sold for the purpose. These are a good economy measure, as they bulk out the paint without changing the colour.

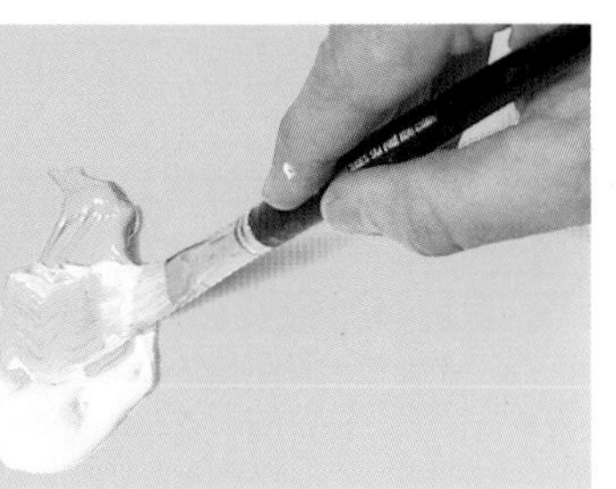

51

KNIFE PAINTING Paint well thickened with impasto medium can be applied with brushes or painting knives. Knives create exciting effects; they press the paint onto the surface, creating flat planes and small ridges at the end of each stroke.

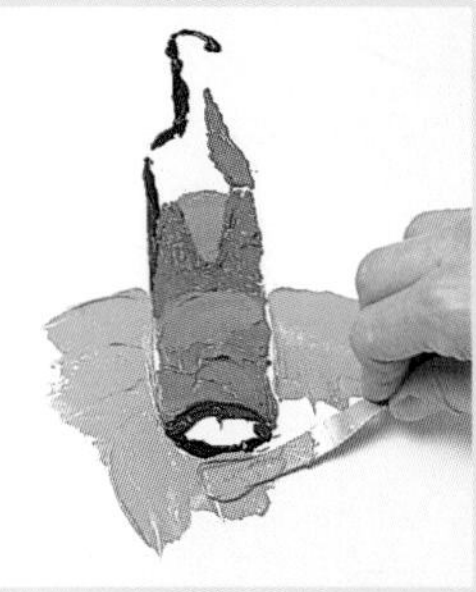

52

RETARDING MEDIUM Because acrylic dries so fast it is difficult to blend thick colours wet-in-wet unless you use retarding medium. This keeps the paint moist for longer so that it remains workable on the surface. It is used with thick paint, not washes, as water affects its action.

53

PAINT TEXTURE Acrylic can be given different textures by mixing it with any one of various special texture mediums. A less costly alternative is to mix it with natural substances – sand or sawdust.

In his painting "Winter Headland" (detail), Robert Tilling has achieved a variety of textures by mixing his paint with sand.

Mixing paint with a special texture medium.

54 **TEXTURED GROUNDS** Interesting effects can also be achieved by texturing the ground, using acrylic modelling paste. You must use a rigid surface for this. Lay the paste on with a knife to create a random rough surface, or press crumpled kitchen foil or relief-patterned objects into it while wet.

Intricate patterns can be built up by scratching into the wet modelling paste.

Pressing any relief-patterned object into the surface leaves an imprint.

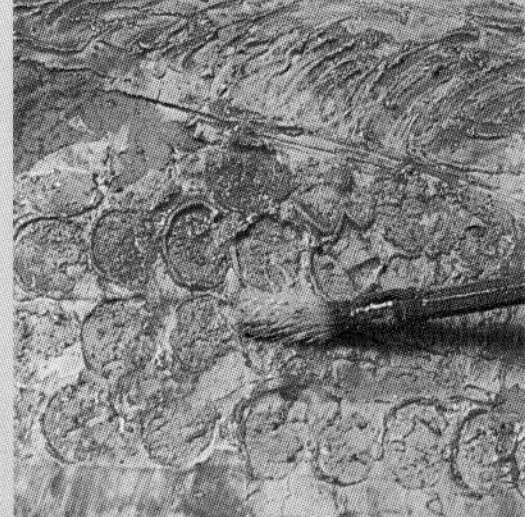

The thick paint catches on the raised ridges, while the diluted yellow-red has collected in the "valleys".

The best effects come from varying the paint consistency so that the underlying pattern shows more in some places than others.

55 EVEN WASHES

Acrylics can be thinned and used like watercolours. To lay a flat wash, choose a large brush and load it as fully as possible with wet paint. Work in even strokes from side to side of the paper, making sure that you pick up the wet edge of the previous stroke each time. If you have a large area to blend, such as a sky getting lighter towards the horizon, try working flat and adding more water to the paint. Use a broad brush to "flow" the colours into each other with rapid, bold strokes.

56 LINE AND WASH

The density of acrylic paint may lead you to overlook its potential for very delicate effects. Used in small quantities and smoothly diluted, it works excellently for the watercolour technique of tinting a pencil or ink drawing.

A line drawing is made first, using a fine pen.

Diluted colour is then brushed in carefully within the pen lines.

The effect is as delicate as watercolour, with the fine pen lines adding a touch of crisp definition.

57 **STAINING** Diluted colour can be applied to primed or raw canvas, with the picture built up in layers of transparent stains. To help the paint adhere and help to eliminate brushmarks either mix the paint with a water-tension breaker or damp the canvas with a solution of water and washing-up liquid.

58 **UNDERPAINTING** Understanding the basic tonal pattern of your painting helps you to key in the colours effectively. Underpainting in monochrome, using a restricted range of tonal values, gives you this important plan. Sketch your subject lightly with the brush, then block in the shadows and mid-tones with thinned paint. You can either retain the key of the picture by then overpainting with washes and glazes, or start to build opaque colour on the underpainted image.

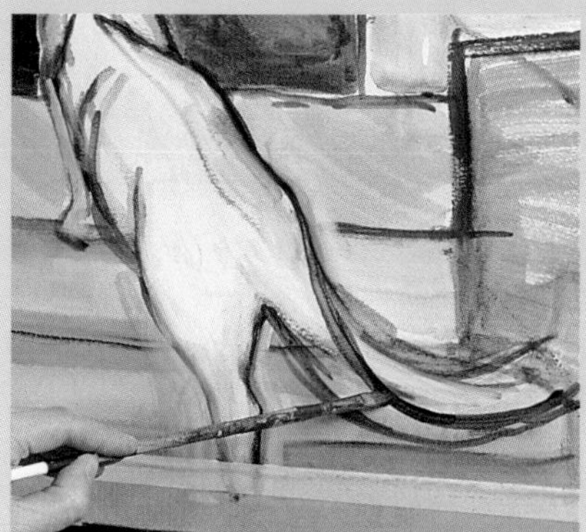

Sketch in your subject using monochrome colours.

The artist has retained the tones in the finished picture.

59 **POINTILLISM** If you have tried the pointillist technique and the colours don't seem to be mixing, it could be because the colours you are using vary too much in tone. To work effectively, the colours used should be the same tone. Use dryish paint, and apply it in short strokes, making sure that the brushstrokes don't blend together.

SURFACE EFFECTS

More than any other paint, acrylic is capable of achieving rich textures that give your painting a lively surface quality. Here you will find some exciting ideas and unconventional methods such as scraping paint onto the surface and mixing acrylic with other media for mixed-media and collage work.

60

DRY BRUSH TECHNIQUE Dry brushing, with either thick or thin paint, creates a broken, dragged texture that is useful for rough or linear textures such as stonework, grass, hair or animal fur. Load the brush with paint, then blot off the excess onto kitchen paper or a rag. Spread the brush bristles and stroke them gently over the working surface.

A base colour is laid thickly, letting the brushmarks show.

Paint is dragged lightly over the surface.

With further layers of colour applied, the texture and pattern are rendered convincingly.

61

SPATTERING Flicked and spattered paint can suggest a specific texture, or simply create contrast for areas of flat colour. For a coarse spatter, load a bristle brush with wet paint and draw your thumb along the top of it. For a fine spray, mix watered paint in a jar and blow it onto the surface with a mouth diffuser. These are made for spraying fixative onto pastel work, and are available in art shops.

Mask out areas not to be spattered.

62

THIN AND THICK Whole pictures can be built up with layers of transparent glazes, or you can vary the surface by glazing over thick impastos. The thin paint slides off the raised areas but runs into the crevices between brush- and knife-strokes to heighten the three-dimensional effect.

Thick paint was used for the hair and allowed to dry. A transparent glaze, made by mixing paint with water and medium, is now applied on top. The effect can be seen in the finished picture (right).

A toothbrush gives a finer spatter.

Paper has been used to merge the spatter drops.

63

SCRAPING Scraping paint onto and across the surface produces thin layers of colour that only partially cover those below. The effect is a little like glazing, but with a livelier surface texture. There are no implements sold for this method, but you can use improvised ones, such as plastic cards.

Using a plastic card, the artist scrapes paint onto paper.

Successive applications build up colours and textures.

64

COMBING Thick paint remains workable for some time, allowing you to work into it to create texture effects. Try dragging a comb through wet colour, or drawing patterns into it with a knife point. Bear in mind, though, that such approaches are best suited to abstract or semi-abstract work.

"Birthday in Edinburgh" by Jacquie Turner.

65

PAINTS AND MEDIUMS At least one manufacturer now produces metallic and iridescent paints and special mediums that help you give excitement and variety to your work. These are worth experimenting with, particularly for collage and mixed-media work.

A drawing is made in charcoal.

Thin paint is used, so the charcoal shows through.

Thicker paint is applied in places.

66 USING CHARCOAL

Charcoal lines give a crisp edge to acrylic painting, but be sure to blow away excess charcoal dust that can contaminate the paint colour. A thin wash of acrylic seals the line drawing onto the surface of canvas or paper.

By varying the consistency of the paint, and drawing with charcoal both under and over the colour, the artist has achieved a lively surface.

67 **WAX RESIST** Because of its regular consistency, even thinned acrylic colour may adhere to and cover a drawing in wax crayon, not giving the resist effect you want. Make a quick test patch and if the paint sticks, add more water.

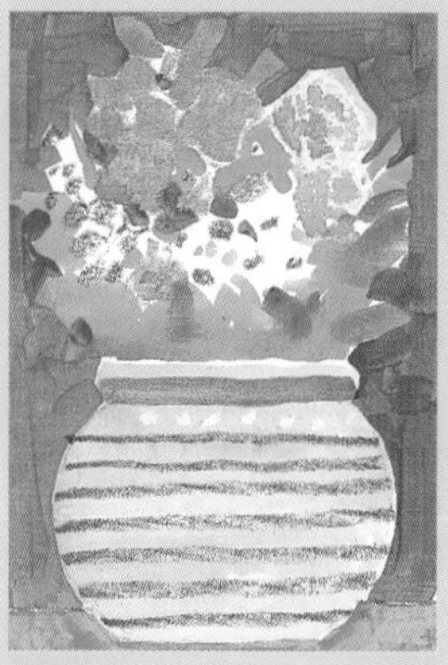

The detail shows where the paint has slid off the waxed areas.

68 **COLLAGE OPTIONS** Because acrylic paints are themselves adhesive, you can add all sorts of collage elements directly to the paint, such as paper scraps, images or textures taken from magazine tear-sheets, and lightweight fabrics, strings and yarns. These can be painted over with thin glazes, if you so wish.

69 **USING PASTEL** Acrylic can be combined with pastel to exploit the different textures; linear strokes or scumbles of pastel contrasting with smoother applications of paint. Soft pastel can be "fixed" with a light application of acrylic medium so that you can build up a painting in layers. Or, use oil pastel, which has better qualities of adherence.

Collage can be used on its own, but is more often combined with paint, as in Mike Bernard's "Road to the Sea". In places, patterned or printed paper has been stuck down and left as it is, while in others (the road in the foreground), thinner paper has been collaged and painted over to create texture.

Oil pastel, used in Helena Greene's "Exmoor", can create exciting resist effects when combined with thinned acrylic.

SUBJECTS

Although there are no "special" ways of painting particular subjects – a landscape and a still life by the same artist will not differ much in style and technique – there are a few subject-related problems, and this chapter shows you some useful "tricks of the trade" for solving them. Rulers and masking tape, for example, are invaluable for helping you achieve straight edges on buildings.

70

VARIED GREENS If you have trouble getting variety into your landscape greens, try creating much more distinct colour contrasts in highlights and shadows. Vibrant yellow, pink or orange can help to light the greens, while true blues and blue-mauves are good shadowing colours. Add them in small touches, and they will "read" as green variations.

In Gerry Baptist's "Life Goes on in Provence" (detail), the overall effect is of rich, varied greens, but in fact there are relatively small areas of pure green, enhanced by the rich, singing blues, oranges and yellows.

71 QUIETER GREENS

Artificial paint colours don't directly match the subtlety of natural greens. If your tube colours look too garish, try mixing in touches of red, red-purple or red-brown. Red is the opposite colour to green and has a subduing influence.

Oxide of chromium

Oxide of chromium + deep violet

Oxide of chromium + raw sienna

72 BRUSHWORK

BRUSHWORK When you are painting trees, look carefully at the growth pattern of branches and leaves and let them guide the direction of your brushwork. Notice whether the foliage canopy sweeps down or fans outward, whether leaves hang from the twigs or push up.

The shapes of the brushmarks describe the foliage on the left.

After blocking in the main shape, the artist begins to define the clumps of foliage.

Notice how the artist established the main shape and slanting thrust of the right-hand tree before dealing with specific areas of foliage. On both trees, the brushmarks follow the directions of the foliage clumps.

The main areas of background foliage are painted initially as solid colour.

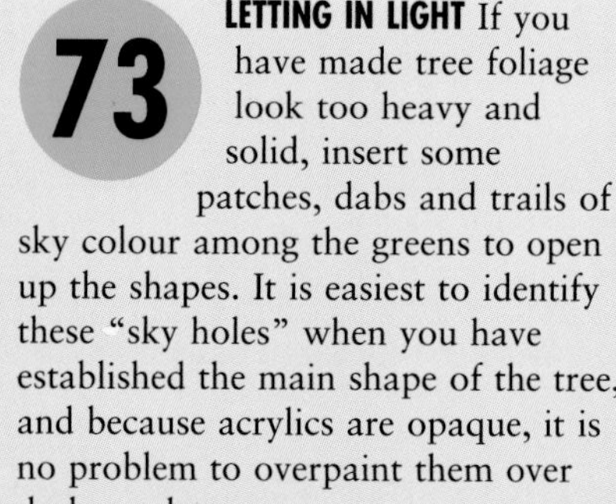

73

LETTING IN LIGHT If you have made tree foliage look too heavy and solid, insert some patches, dabs and trails of sky colour among the greens to open up the shapes. It is easiest to identify these "sky holes" when you have established the main shape of the tree, and because acrylics are opaque, it is no problem to overpaint them over darker colours.

Trunks and branches are defined by painting light colours around and between the shapes.

Finally, the colours were deepened and enriched with glazes.

74

REGULAR PATTERNS On buildings, use a flat brush to create the patterns of brickwork or roof tiles – choose one that is the right width to paint each rectangle boldly in one stroke. Use shorter strokes to add shading or highlighting to the shapes.

Alan Oliver has used a similar technique in his "Winter's Morning", painting sky colour lightly over the colours used for the background trees.

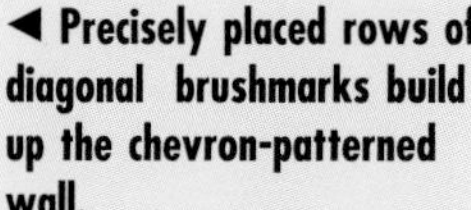

◄ Precisely placed rows of diagonal brushmarks build up the chevron-patterned wall.

On the wall, care was taken to gradually reduce the size of the brushmarks, creating the effect of the receding plane.

Put masking tape on area to be masked.

75

MASKING A wobbly or tilting edge on the walls or windows of a building can spoil the effect, so if clean straight lines are important to your painting, use masking tape to harden the edges of main shapes and brush ruling for straight-line details.

Apply paint along edge of the tape.

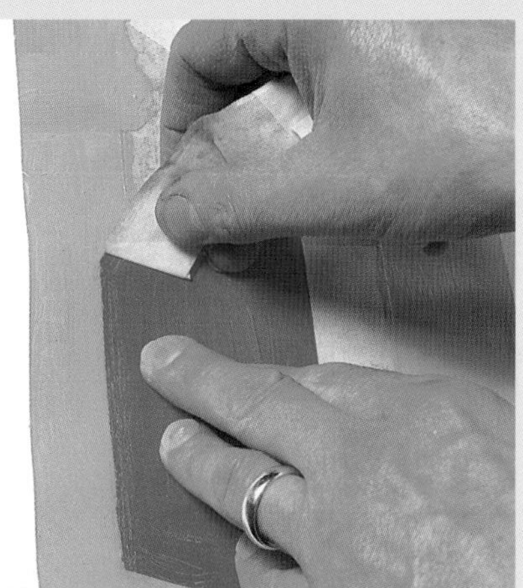

Peel off masking tape to reveal a straight edge.

76

ONE-STROKE TOUCHES Distant houses or cottages in landscape can be simply touched in using a flat brush in one decisive stroke.

77 CHECKING ACCURACY

CHECKING ACCURACY When painting an architectural subject that has straight lines and hard angles, stand back from the painting frequently to check that verticals and horizontals are accurate. Hold up a ruler with your arm out straight and align it to the painted shapes. If you keep working close to the image, wrongly angled brush strokes can push parts of the subject out of line.

78 EDGE QUALITIES

EDGE QUALITIES In still life painting, bear in mind that objects do not really have outlines, we perceive a line where one surface overlaps or turns against another. The edge quality may be indistinct in parts, for example if the colour or tone is similar, so it should not be painted as a hard divide. By contrast, another part may appear sharply defined. The contrast of "lost and found" edges gives a sense of reality.

In Paul Powis's "Jugs", the two vessels on the left merge into one another, while in the centre – also the picture's centre of interest – the edges are sharp and clear.

79

HIGHLIGHTS The shinier a surface is, the more intense its highlights. If you are painting a glass or white-metal object don't be afraid to make strong highlights really dazzling – apply thick, opaque, pure white paint.

The artist begins with a mid-blue, to which she will add darker and lighter colours.

This curving highlight is put on after the band of shadow beneath, using thick paint.

The small highlights where the jug catches direct light are almost pure white. These were added last.

On a shiny, rounded surface the pattern of highlights can be quite intricate, resulting in a wide variety of colours.

Main shape blocked in.

Dark tone added to edges.

Highlights added.

The foot of the bottle reflects darker colour, with little of the yellow visible.

80 GLASS

Because glass is both transparent and reflective, it often presents confusing layers of information that are difficult to sort out. Try first looking through the glass to see shapes created by the background colours, and block them in quite broadly. Then, look for highlights and dark tones that define the form of the object itself; these typically fall on edges, angles and curves, giving definition to the shapes.

81

HIGHLIGHT COLOURS A common mistake in painting pale skin is to make the highlights too light, resulting in a painting that is too high in "key". You can check the tone of highlights by holding up a piece of white card in front of the subject; this will show you that they are nowhere near white.

In Daniel Stedman's "Fleur, Dancer Backlit", the highlights on face and chest stand out dramatically against the dark tones, but are nowhere near pure white.

82

DIRECTIONAL BRUSHWORK Look for the main forms when you are painting a figure and let your brushstrokes follow them, using long strokes for legs, arms, and the folds of clothing or drapery, and shorter curves for rounded forms.

In Daniel Stedman's "Julie", brushwork plays a vital role in describing the shapes and forms.

83

HAIR TEXTURES Dry brushing is an excellent technique for painting animal hair or fur. Use a strong bristle brush for coarse hair, a nylon brush for a softer effect. Paint the texture over a base coat of flat colour. If you want to add fine lines representing individual hairs or whiskers, use a narrow, round brush and paint with the tip.

A soft brush is used to drag thick colour over a dry underlayer.

The effect of the long, shaggy coat is built up with brushmarks in different directions.

You can see the dry-brush effect clearly around the neck and haunches; the paint does not completely cover the colours beneath.

REMEDIAL METHODS

One of the great attractions of acrylic is that you can make corrections in a number of ways without damaging the picture surface; this makes it the ideal medium for the beginner. If you are using thick, opaque paint you can simply overpaint any mistakes, while colours can be amended by glazing over them.

84

CLEAN EDGES If you are trying to paint to an outline and your brush wobbles over the edge, use the side of your thumb to gently "push" the colour back into place.

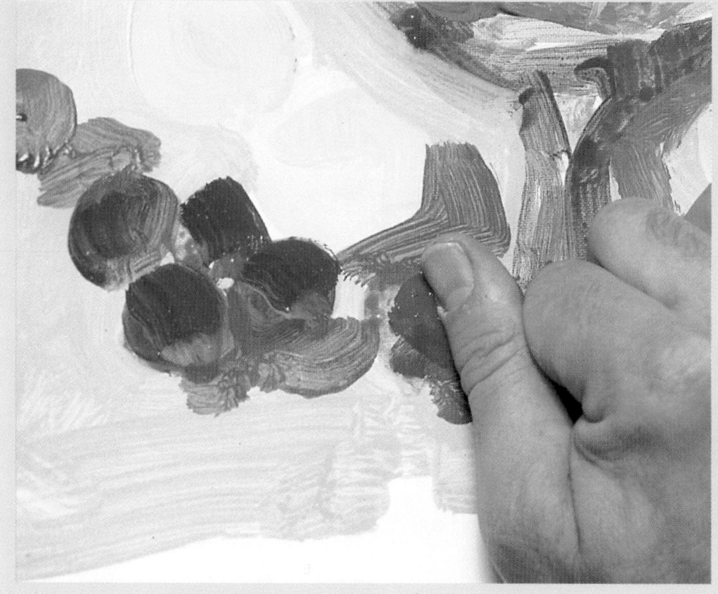

While still wet, the paint can be moved around with fingers or thumbs, but do not attempt this if it has begun to dry.

The onions are painted wet-in-wet to create soft blends.

The work is assessed.

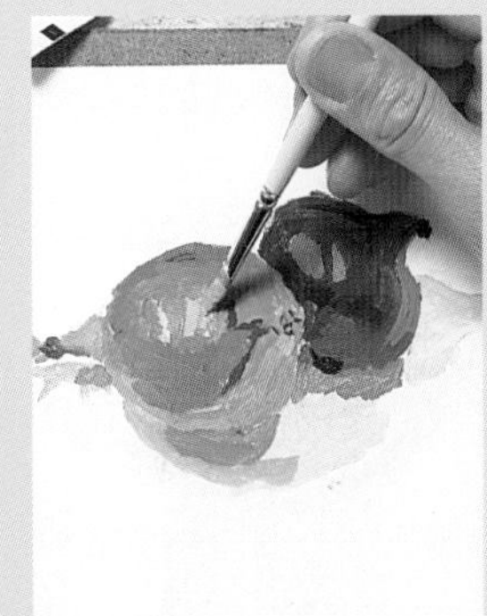

When the painting is dry, the highlights are overpainted.

85 WHEN TO STOP

Avoid over-working your colours when making corrections. If you make successive, rapid changes working wet-into-wet, you will start to get a smeared, muddy surface. At this point, it is best to leave the painting to dry. When you come back to it, you can overpaint cleanly on the sealed surface. Bringing a fresh eye to your work may also suggest a different solution.

86

BLOCKING OUT To rework individual shapes and details, simply block them out with a layer of opaque white paint, giving yourself a clean ground for the revision. This method can also help you to make bold decisions about colour changes that might lift a dull picture.

A yellow shape was tried out in the background to balance the foreground fruit.

However, the artist decided against this, and so overpaints the area with thick white paint before proceeding further.

87

PATCHING If a particular area of your painting has gone disastrously wrong but you are pleased with all the rest, you can stick on a patch of clean paper using an acrylic-based adhesive. Redraw that part of your subject and build up the colours gradually, taking the fresh paint over the edges of the patch to fill the join.

REMOVING PAINT If you want to use a palette knife to scrape back an error or remove some too-thick paint, make your decision quickly before it really starts to dry. Once the plastic skin has formed, the paint will peel away raggedly and may form a rough edge that cannot be overpainted cleanly.

The original choice of colour-scheme is blue-green and pink.

The jug's shape is strengthened with dark outlines.

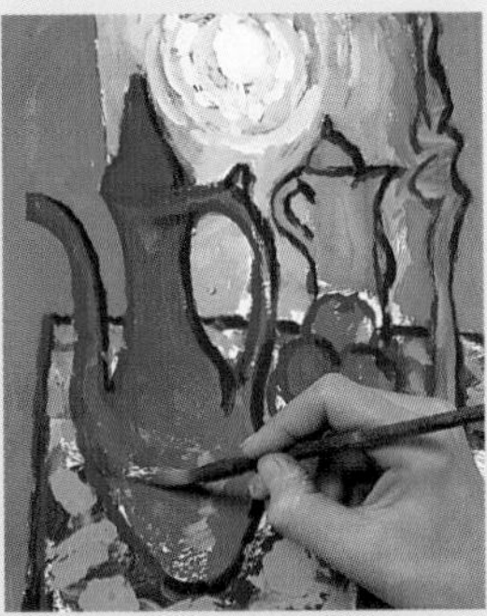

Having added the light, the artist works on the jug.

89 TRYING AGAIN

Don't throw away a composition that has gone wrong – use it as a learning tool to help you get it right on a second try. Draw with a brush over the shapes and colours that you previously put down, using them as your guide for improving the image. If you always start from scratch, it's easy to repeat the same kind of errors.

In the final stages the picture was radically changed, with the objects now appearing in dark semi-silhouette against the glowing light.

Water-diluted paint is glazed over the foreground.

90 COLOUR BALANCE

You can heighten the overall mood of a painting by putting on a final colour glaze. For example, a landscape that is not sufficiently sunny can be glazed over thinly with bright yellow; a cosy interior can be bathed in a red glow. Lay the painting flat while you brush on the thinned paint, and let it dry flat to avoid runs and dribbles.

The foreground glaze has strengthened the colour as well as softening the boundaries between sunlight and shadows.

CRAFT HINTS

Acrylics are tough and highly versatile, and can be used on a wide variety of surfaces, which makes them ideal for decorating a range of household objects, clothing and children's toys. For shiny surfaces such as glass, you may need to buy a special type of paint, as the normal acrylics are not designed for this purpose, and will not adhere well. Ask for information in your art or craft shop.

91 CRAFT ACRYLICS

For craft projects such as decorative painting and stencilling onto wood, fabrics, paper, cardboard, plastic, papier-mâché or ceramics, special acrylic craft paints are available. These work on all surfaces. Normal artist's acrylics can be used in some craft work though they are not advised for use on non-absorbent surfaces, like ceramics, nor highly absorbent ones. If you're using artist's acrylics on wood, seal the wood first.

92 **WOODEN TOYS** Simple wooden toys can be easily coloured with acrylic paints, but make sure the paints are non-toxic – check the tube or bottle labels or ask for paint information sheets. Use the paint fairly thickly to build up an opaque surface and add details when the paint is dry. When complete, the toy can be varnished with one of the available finishes.

93 **PICTURE FRAMES** Acrylics can be used to give old picture frames a further lease of life or new ones a different surface colour. Sand lightly to help the paint adhere to the surface then apply a layer of acrylic gesso and allow to dry. Work each side separately, covering the corners with masking tape along the mitred joint. The paint should be thinned and put on with a wide brush to give a dragged-paint effect. To highlight parts of the frame, wipe carefully with a rag while the paint is still wet. Remove the tape and allow to dry thoroughly before treating the remaining sides.

Apply gesso glaze, leave to dry then stick masking tape over one of the mitres.

Apply acrylic paint, using long strokes to "drag" the surface evenly.

Wipe paint from some of the mouldings. Leave to dry. Repeat for other two sides.

94 DECORATIVE TERRA COTTA

Liven up an old plant pot by decorating it with acrylic paints. If you plan to grow plants in the pots then leave some of the surface area unpainted, otherwise the painted surface will deteriorate when the plant is watered.

95

PEARLIZED ACRYLIC INKS These shimmering colours can be used on glass, ceramic, wood, paper and board. They are water resistant, though if you have painted a ceramic item you should wash it by hand, and with care.

96

THIN FABRICS Acrylic paint can come through a thin fabric, so if you are painting a garment such as a T-shirt, place a piece of clean card between the two layers so that the paint is only absorbed by the layer on which you are working. This will also provide a firm surface on which to paint.

97

PREPARING FABRICS Whether stencilling or painting fabrics, such as canvas, it is important to wash the fabric first so that any size is removed; this may hinder paint absorption. If the fabric becomes too soft, it can be starched when the decoration is completed. If you are decorating a large area, say, curtains, before starting test the paint on the wrong side of the fabric or on a spare piece.

Before you begin painting, on a spare piece of fabric, test out the design, the colour of the paints, and the absorbency of the fabric.

98 PAINTING PAPIER-MACHE

Acrylic paints give a strong, solid flat finish to papier-mâché, which can then be varnished. If using a light base colour, cover the papier-mâché with a coat of white emulsion or gesso to prevent the newsprint showing through. The design details here have been added with a black fine-pointed permanent marker.

99 PAINT AND GLITTER

This shell has been decorated with a combination of pearlized paint, glitter and gilt. You can buy ready-made blank plaster casts from craft shops. You could try making a set of shells, pearlized in different colours using the gilded finish to link them as a set.

Brush on the pearlized paint.

Before the paint dries, sprinkle on the glitter.

Draw your design on a piece of paper and put it inside the jar.

Paint onto the glass following the paper pattern.

The finished cookie jar.

100

PAINTED GLASS You can make an art object out of a plain glass bottle or storage container by painting a design on the outside. Cut a piece of paper which will fit inside the container, draw the design on this, and stick it firmly to the inside of the container to act as a guide.

Apply highlights of gold gilding wax along the ridges of the shell.

CREDITS

The author would like to acknowledge the invaluable hints and tips given by the following artists and experts while researching this book: Mrs. G. Barwick; John S. Bowman; J. Lockheart Davidson; Gordana Bjelic-Rados. Thanks also to Vivien Frank who wrote the craft tips.

Quarto would like to thank David Cuthbert, Jeremy Galton, Ian Sidaway and Hazel Harrison for demonstrating the art techniques; and Ron Fuller, Jackie Schou and Sarah Doe for the craft tips.

Quarto would also like to thank Daler-Rowney who supplied the artist's materials; Maestro Craft Colours Ltd. for the craft paints; Spectrum Oil Colours, London, SW19, for pigments for mixing your own paints.

Art editor Clare Baggaley
Designer Tanya Devonshire-Jones
Photographers Laura Wickenden, Colin Bowling
Text editor Hazel Harrison
Senior editor Kate Kirby
Picture researcher Jo Carlill
Picture manager Giulia Hetherington
Editorial director Mark Dartford
Art director Moira Clinch

Typeset by Genesis Typesetting, Rochester
Manufactured in Hong Kong by Regent Publishing Services Ltd.
Printed in China by Leefung-Asco Printers Ltd.